Stop Yelling

Parenting Tips and Tricks on How to Stop Yelling at Your Kids, Stay Calm and Reduce Stress Today

Amelia Farris

www.southshorepublications.com

ISBN-13: 978-1517259174

ISBN-10: 1517259177

CONTENTS

INTRODUCTION

Do you find yourself losing your temper far more often that you would like? Do you find yourself yelling far more than you ever thought you would? Well, parenting is probably the hardest and most demanding job you can ever undertake, so you're not alone in feeling that way.

We all have a breaking point where we snap and lose our temper with people. Often the people we love most are on the receiving end, this includes our children. Somehow kids seem to have a way of really pushing our buttons from time to time, testing the patience of even the calmest parents among us. So you shouldn't feel bad for snapping and yelling every once in a while. However, when the yelling becomes a common occurrence, problems start to emerge.

The information in this book is perfect for parents who lose their temper with their kids, however this information also applies to everyone in your life. If you find you are losing your temper with other people, the ideas and techniques we are going to talk about can be applies to these scenarios too. So by learning the information in this book, you will also be improving your other relationships and the way you react to conflict and arguments in all areas of your life. This is a very valuable skill to have.

If you get angry too often then your loved ones will start to distance themselves from you, either consciously or subconsciously without even realizing it. They will begin to associate you with stress and negative experiences and emotions and they will enjoy being around you less and less as time goes on. Combine this with the discipline you are giving to your children when they are misbehaving, this creates a lot of negativity in your relationship. We are going to talk about exactly how to turn this around.

So it's important that we keep calm and lose our temper most of the time, only losing our temper in extreme circumstances when people really cross the line. It's no good throwing a huge tantrum every time someone does something slightly wrong. If you do, you will push people away and make them simply not like you! But this does happen a lot, because those small everyday issues are often the ones that get us the most irritated.

Sometimes, because of the way we perceive things, we may become angry and want to yell at someone who doesn't deserve to be yelled at. This is just due to the fact that we are looking at things in the wrong way completely, which we will look into in more detail and talk about changing that mindset for good.

Aside from not pushing people away and having them not want to spend time with you, staying calm and being less stressed is also going to be beneficial for you and your health. Stress has a lot of major effects on the body, which I will go into in more detail. It's important that you recognize exactly what stress is doing to you so that you understand how vital keeping calm really is.

That's really what the aim is here, it's not to simply stop yelling at your kids and other people in your life, it's to actually stop you wanting to yell. It's no good just papering over the cracks by just helping you to stop verbalizing your emotions. Expressing how you feel is a good thing, we just need to stop is happening in such an extreme, anger infused way. The way we are going to do this is change by changing the way you think in order to stop you feeling those strong emotions of anger that lead you to start yelling at people.

I understand that discipline is important, but it doesn't always have to mean losing your temper and showing your kid that they have done wrong by telling them off. There are other forms of discipline that you can use that will enable you to teach your children right and wrong while correcting their behavior in a positive way, which we will discuss in detail.

If you utilize the information in this book, you will be able to build much closer and more loving connections with those around you. You will also be able to cut out a lot of manipulation that we all use to get what we want and get our kids to act the way we want them to sometimes. We can also reduce the amount of threats that we need to dish out to our kids. All of this will provide the basis for a very happy and low stress family life that you can start working towards as soon as you finish this book. So, turn over the page and we'll get started!

WHY DO WE YELL?

Well, I think it's fairly obvious nobody wants to yell. So why do we end up doing it? There are three main reasons that we end up resorting to yelling at our children, which I will cover in this first chapter. Hopefully after this chapter you will have a better understanding of why you start yelling, because we may not even realize the exact reasons ourselves sometimes.

Frustration

Getting frustrated with your kids is something that happens to all of us, usually fairly regularly. They may have a habit of doing something that we just get sick and tired of after a while. Or maybe we just get frustrated with having to keep asking them to do something or to not do something, only for them to just not listen to us no matter how hard we try!

Having to put up with this kind of thing is enough to make even the calmest person in the world get frustrated. What you will notice is that if this is happening and they aren't listening to you, is that every time you ask them to do something and they don't do it, you will raise your voice a little higher. The more frustrated you get, the louder your voice gets.

So let's say you're telling them to stop doing something that they shouldn't be doing. So you say, "Stop doing that." But they don't listen. What do you do next? You say it in a more stern tone. Then if they still don't listen you maybe start elaborating a bit, all the time growing more frustrated that they are still doing it even though you're telling them to stop. The stress is building and you're getting so frustrated until you yell at them to, "Stop that right now!"

Sound familiar? I'm sure it does to every single person reading this book. It's a very common occurrence and it's a direct result of simple frustration.

Being Judged

Many parents will get angry and yell at their children when in company due to the thought that they are being judged based on their children's actions. So you may feel like people are watching how your child is acting and if they do something wrong, that it's a reflection on you as a parent.

So what do you do to compensate for these thoughts? You visibly and loudly discipline your child for everyone to see so that it looks like you don't condone the bad behavior, just to make sure everyone knows.

The strange thing about this is that the same action can be done by your child and by someone else's child and your reaction would be completely different. If someone else's child did it, your reaction would probably be pretty normal. Then if your child does exactly the same thing, you end up shouting at them.

So for example let's say you have a friend round and they bring their child with them. Their child then sits and plays with your child while you both talk. Then their child accidentally knocks over a cup and spills a drink on your floor. Your reaction would probably be to rush to clean it up, but then you would tell them that it's okay and accidents happen or something to that effect.

Now, let's take the exact same scenario but flip it round. So let's say you have taken your child to your friend's house and they spill a drink on your friends floor. Would your reaction be to tell them that 'accidents happen'? Or would it be to get annoyed and tell them off for being so clumsy and not paying enough attention?

Almost always it's going to be the latter. If you really think about it, you're not telling your child off for the sake of the child, you're doing it to make it seem like the spill wasn't your fault and that this is not behavior that you tolerate. Your instant thought when the spill happens is how your friend will be reacting to this happening and so you go into angry parent mode and tell your child off because it's what you think your friend would expect you to do, not because you genuinely think they need to be told off to that extent.

This is a tricky one that most people don't really think about, so keep an eye out for it and recognize when you are yelling at your child for other peoples benefit.

Learned Yelling

The final reason why people generally yell at their kids is because you have simply learned to do it from a young age. If your parents yelled at you a lot when you were younger, it's something that will probably come pretty naturally to you and you will be more likely to raise your voice to your kids. If yelling is just something that comes naturally to you because of your upbringing, you are going to really have to work to break this cycle and we will talk more about how to do this later in the book.

WHAT DOES YELLING DO?

Yelling at our kids does a few things. It mostly depends on the type of child, as different types of child will react to it differently, which I will go into, but it also has a couple of other negative side effects.

Well Behaved Children

What I mean by well-behaved children, are the type of kids that will generally do what you tell them. They won't constantly be running around being noisy or messy and they will usually do what you ask them.

If you have a child that's more towards the 'good' and 'well behaved' end of the spectrum, shouting is simply futile. Children that are well behaved are doing it through choice. They generally make the choice to be well behaved as they want to please you. So shouting at a child that wants to please you anyway because they made a mistake is not going to have any positive effect what so ever.

In this situation, yelling will serve to do nothing other than make a child with this kind of mindset sad and feel like they are failing to make you happy, even though that's what they are trying to do. If you do have a well behaved child, just to keep in mind that they are well behaved because they choose to be and they want validation from you that they are pleasing you. So yelling at them for silly reasons can be very detrimental and hurtful to them.

Naughty Children

When I say 'naughty children' I'm referring to the type of child that will generally be disruptive, hit or kick his or her siblings to get a reaction, try to get more attention and not do what they are told.

With children that aren't generally so well behaved, shouting at them is basically giving them what they want. They want you to give them attention and notice them. The easiest way to do this is to drive you up the wall! Then when you yell at them and they force you to take action, they have got your attention and they have won.

Children are pretty much immune to yelling, they don't mind it and it doesn't stress them out. All yelling does is basically say 'you have my full attention now' so you're giving them what they want and rewarding them with attention in return for bed behavior.

Pushing People Away

What shouting will definitely do is push people away and make them not want to be around you. Obviously your children will see you as being more of a mean person but they aren't going anywhere until they're old enough to fly the next so you can't physically push them away with your yelling just yet. Other people however, that's a different story.

If you are constantly shouting at your children in the presence of other people, you can quite easily make them not want to be around you. This is a big cause of marital issues that affect couples with children. If your partner sees you as this stressed, loud, angry person, they will be far more likely to want to get away from you and away from the house completely in some cases just to get some peace and quiet.

This can commonly lead to a breakdown in communication, which is a massive marriage killer, because who wants to try and talk to someone who is just constantly getting stressed and yelling when something happens that they don't like. It's only natural to not want to talk to someone like that, even if they do feel like they have a good reason to yell a lot of the time.

Also family and friends will obviously not like to be around someone who yells at their kids far too much. It's just generally quite an awkward experience for onlookers as someone yells and disciplines their child in front of them. For parents it sometimes seems normal to yell at a child then carry on talking normally to someone else as if nothing happened, but to a lot of people it's pretty strange behavior, especially if they don't have kids themselves. They won't want to be around that kind of thing as it's just not a pleasant experience.

Too Much Information

A very common problem with letting your anger get the better of you and having a shouting match with your kids is that you will say things you don't mean.

This generally only happens if your child is argumentative and shouting back at you, but it does happen, especially as they get a bit older and start to learn hurtful things to say to you in an argument.

As I'm sure you will know from previous arguments throughout your life, when people argue, they say things they don't mean. Sometimes very extreme things that they don't mean. For example, I have heard more than one story about parents saying something about wish they hadn't had a child when angry, which they obviously don't mean, but this can be very detrimental none the less.

Just because you know you don't mean something and it was just something you said in the heat of the moment, those words will stick in your child's head for a long time. So it's very important that we don't let this happen and we get our stress and anger under control as soon as possible.

WHAT IS STRESS DOING TO YOU?

So now you know what yelling and stress can do to your relationships with other people, how about what it can do to your body? As I said in the introduction, it's important to understand what stress is doing to you so that you realize the importance of keeping your stress levels down.

Just this information alone can be enough to help you calm yourself when you feel like you're getting angry. Simply knowing how the stress you are feeling is effecting you is a big incentive to calm yourself without even having any advanced techniques to help, so this is an important chapter to read.

Fight or Flight

Your body will be in a heightened state of readiness when you experience stress. This is called the fight or flight mechanism and it's meant to get us ready to either fight and deal with the danger, or run and get away from it.

This system is only designed to be working while we deal with a threat and then shut off again once the situation is over. But if you're stressed, worried and anxious, this system stays on inside us for extended periods of time. This can cause us some serious issues if left unchecked.

Blood Pressure

The fight of flight mechanism will cause our heart to speed up and beat harder. This means it will be working overtime in order to get blood to our muscles during times of anxiety. This in turn puts your blood pressure up as your heart is pumping your blood faster and harder. As I'm sure you know, over extended periods of time, high blood pressure can lead to heart attacks and heart disease. High blood pressure can also cause the cells in your blood to stick together more than usual. This can lead to blood clots which cause strokes.

Immune System

Just being stressed will cause your immune system to not work as effectively as it should do. Prolonged periods of stress and heightened flight or fight response will lead to decreased immunity in your body.

This is because when you are under stress, your immune system is suppressed. This means you are more likely to get ill more often and have even more symptoms that will cause you to stress even more! It really is a vicious cycle.

Digestive System

Similarly, your digestive system will also be suppressed. This happens because the fight or flight response is diverting your blood flow to your muscles, where it think it's needed most. So the reduced flow of blood to your digestive system means that it becomes suppressed.

This can lead to weight gain and obesity over extended periods of time, which can in turn cause a host of other health issues. Also, if you get acid reflux a lot, this could be due to reduced digestive system function as a direct result of being stressed.

Blood Sugar

Surprisingly enough, stress actually increases your blood sugar levels. High blood sugar can lead to a whole range of issues including, diabetes, nerve damage and even problems with your eye sight.

Other Effects

Stress can also cause premature aging, a reduced sex drive, reduced sex function, infertility and a range of other issues too long to go into in this chapter! Just having stress hormones in your system on a regular basis can lead to insomnia and a very disrupted sleep pattern, memory and concentration issues, addiction and depression.

So as you can see, stress is a really serious issue that we need to get under control as quickly as possible. Many of these problems only become an issue when stress is left unchecked for a very extended period of time, so as long as you take action on the advice that's to follow, you can help yourself avoid all of these potential problems.

STOP YELLING

Now for the moment you have all been waiting for, some techniques that we can implement to stop feeling so angry and stressed and some ways to actually stop yelling.

Track Your Yelling

The first thing you should do is start making a note every time you yell. This will let you figure out exactly what the main causes and reasons there are behind the yelling and it will help you to identify things you may not otherwise realize. So there are a few specific things you should make a note of in order to identify trends.

There are two main things that you really need to make a note of when you are recording this information. The first thing is the cause, or what made you feel like you wanted to yell. The second is what you wanted to achieve by yelling, or what is the outcome that you thought yelling would help you get to.

This will enable to you really notice any patterns in your yelling and identify the most problematic areas. You can also look for times and situations that cause you to yell the most. For example, do you yell most in the mornings. If so, is this because you're over tired? Maybe you get stressed and yell more often at a certain time of day, which could be something to do with your eating habits. Having low blood sugar can cause a lower tolerance to stress and cause you to yell more often for example.

Take Control of Your Reactions

Your reaction is your immediate response to a trigger. So for example, a trigger could be when your child hits their brother or sister. This will obviously make you feel angry, then comes the reaction.

Your reaction is usually instant and you don't even have time to consider carefully what you are going to do. You just react in the way that you always do out of habit and instinct without thinking. So you essentially aren't using self-control to govern your reaction to this trigger and the reaction that you have could quite easily be yelling.

What you need to do to stop the yelling in this situation is to stop yourself and control your reaction for a moment. The best way to do this is to just stop for a moment and take a breath before reacting. Just doing this can really help you to react in a much more controlled way.

If you allow your anger and immediate reaction to take over, you are just going to keep repeating the same behavior as you always have done and you will end up yelling, so this is a really important step. Control the reaction and think it through.

Have a Plan

It helps to know how you want to react in any given situation. This will allow you to react to triggers in a much better way in future. So, to do this we need to refer back to our list we made.

On this list, you will have the cause and what you wanted to achieve with your reaction. Now if you look at this and carefully consider what the best course of action would be in future, you will be better prepared to deal with it when it happens again.

If you have thought this through properly, you will know what to do and your brain will have an instant option or course of action other than your usual response of yelling. This really helps with the reaction control process, as you will be able to react in the perfect, pre-thought out way every time this issue arises.

TIPS AND TRICKS

So we have the main process covered and we know why stopping our yelling is so important. The method I described in the last chapter is the best way to really cut down on the yelling. However, there are some very clever little tips and tricks I can give you to help you along the way. Some of these very simple little changes really are quite brilliant and can help you cut down on the yelling with very little effort from day one.

Imagine You're Being Watched

Once you get in to the habit of doing this one, it's not even something you have to think about. All you have to do is to imagine someone is watching you who you wouldn't want to shout and make a scene in front of.

So this could be a nosy neighbor that you wouldn't want to see you screaming at your kids as you would find it embarrassing, it could be your child's school teacher or even a family member. You could even imagine a group of people if you like, it's completely up to you.

Now whenever you feel like you're getting angry and you want to yell, try to remember to imagine you're being watched. This might be hard to begin with because when you're that angry, there's not a whole lot else you will be able to focus on, but once you have remembered a few times this will start to be an automatic thought. You will notice that when you begin to yell, or just after you yell, you will start to get the feeling of being watched and stop automatically.

I found this little trick particularly helpful in my own family life. I also use this technique for other purposes too such as, if the house is getting dirty, I will imagine what other people would think if they could see it and see me just sitting there not tidying. This definitely motivates me to get busy cleaning the place up rather than just leaving it.

Learning Opportunities

A great mindset to employ is to view each time that your child misbehaves as a learning opportunity. After all, the bad behavior they are displaying is essentially a mistake. Mistakes are there to be corrected and to correct your child you need to teach them. You have to teach them why what they are doing is wrong and what they should be doing instead.

So really try to get this across to them in a rational way rather than just allowing yourself to become angry. If you really start to try understanding the reason behind the behavior and tackle it in a logical way rather than just yelling, you won't even feel the need to yell as much because this far more understanding mindset offers you another option that is a lot more appealing.

Cut Out Non-Angry Yelling

After a while, if you yell too much, it will lose all effectiveness anyway. People become desensitized to anything if they are exposed to it enough. So don't just try to yell less when you are mad. You should also try to cut out raising the volume if your voice needlessly in everyday situations.

So for example, if you need to speak to someone who is in a different room, don't shout from room to room. Although it's more effort, try walking in the room and talking to them from now on instead. This overall lower volume will be picked up on by everyone in the house and this will do two main things for you.

Firstly, when you lower the volume if your voice, so will everyone else. This might not happen right away, but your family members will subconsciously pick up on it and begin to speak more quietly themselves. Although you shouldn't expect miracles with this, it will be a subtle change, but it will happen. This will obviously help your home to be a more pleasant and peaceful place to be for everyone that lives there and everyone who visits too.

The second thing this will do is that when you do raise your voice, even slightly, everyone will pay attention without you having to resort to yelling at them. You will even feel strange about yelling if you haven't done it in a while.

You have to remember that yelling at your family members isn't an everyday occurrence for most people and when it does happen, it's a big deal. Yelling loses all meaning when it happens a lot and when it just happens because everyone is so used to it. So if you want raising your voice to actually mean something again, this technique is definitely for you.

Pick Your Battles

You should always remember, you don't have to turn up to every single fight that you're invited to. Even if you're half way through a yelling match with a member of your family, you can walk away at any time. This simple fact seems to be lost on many parents, probably out of stubbornness or simply wanting to have the last word seeing as you're the adult.

The fact is, if you walk away, you will simply be able to resolve things in a much more calm way when you have both had the chance to think things through. This is obviously a much more rational way of doing things, so try it when things are getting out of hand.

As a parent in particular, you are expected to be the bigger person and resolve the conflict in the best possible way. So even if your child is being disrespectful and saying hurtful things, just walking away from them is a very powerful thing to do. This is often a much more powerful statement than yelling back at them.

By walking away, especially if you don't normally do this, it will actually make a very big impression. It will also give them time to think about what exactly they said to make you walk off. This gives them time to reflect on their words and really reflect on just how hurtful the things they said were. This will usually lead to them feeling guilty and not wanting to do it again, which is the ideal end result, and it's all achieved simply by walking away when things are getting a bit out of hand.

Talk to Your Partner

If you have a partner who you are raising your kids with, talk to them about how you are feeling with regards to the yelling. If you are yelling a lot, you can be pretty certain that they have noticed it. If you bring it up and talk to them about it, at least they will know that you realize you are doing it and want to do something about it.

They may have some suggestions as they know the inner workings of your family better than anyone else, so they are the ideal person to discuss this kind of thing with. They may also be able to help out with some of the situations that cause you the most stress and cause you to yell the most.

You may be surprised by the effect that simply telling them how your feeling may have on the situation. Just the fact that you're asking them for help, which a lot of couples seems to refuse to do these days, will often make them respond in a positive, understanding and helpful way.

POSITIVE DISCIPLINE

Discipline is very important and just because you won't be yelling so much, this doesn't mean you can't discipline as much as you would like to. Yelling and spanking are two forms of negative discipline which aren't exactly the most tactile or recommended of methods to say the least. So instead we can use positive discipline to teach our children about better behavior.

Just because you have to hold back and control your temper, doesn't mean you should be less strict with your kids or start letting them win when they are misbehaving. This will only lead to more problems down the line as they get older and they think they can get away with whatever they like because you let them win when they were kids.

It's really important to keep this in mind. Right now, your child might be drawing on the walls with crayons and getting away with it, but give it a few years and this kind of mentality can easily turn into underage drinking and smoking for example. That probably sounds extreme but what we teach them when they are young really does reflect very strongly on their personalities as they grow into teenagers.

What is Positive Discipline

The general way of showing your kids right and wrong is of course to punish them when they misbehave and reward them when they are good.

The problem with punishing kids when they are bad is that punishments such as yelling, spanking, sending them to their room, grounding them, etc. come with a lot of negative side effects. Children can grow very resentful of this indeed. I have seen cases where kids will refuse to speak to their parents for years because they felt like they were disciplined too much as kids. Essentially, discipline breaks down the bond between the parent and child by bringing negativity into their relationship on a regular basis.

So how do you discipline them and show them that they have done wrong without the negative side effects? Well, with positive discipline, what we are trying to achieve is children having their own sense of self-control over their own behavior. This is an important step, because when we constantly provide them with reward and punishment throughout their whole lives, when that system is taken away, it can be harder for them to make their own choices as to what is right and wrong. They will still know and understand what's right and wrong no matter what, but seeing as the reward and consequence has gone, they may start to make the wrong decisions.

So if we get them started making their own decisions with low risk of being punished for doing something bad from a young age, they will be much better equipped when they meet tough choices later in life and they have the opportunity to do something bad. They are far more likely to make the right choice based on their own self-control using this technique.

This positive discipline method has a lot to do with respect. You must both gain your child's respect but you must also show them respect in return and treat them like a person and not as a naughty kid that needs to be told off. This is important because, by simply showing your child respect, they will give it back in return. If you don't respect them however, then they won't respect you back. It's that simple.

Many parents believe that respect is a one way street and that, just because they are older than the child and the child is living under their roof, they have to do whatever their parents tell them without question. Well the main problem with that kind of thinking is that your kids will feel like they are prisoners or slaves. Why would they respect anyone who makes them feel that way? You have to remember that they are human beings with their own minds, not just a child that has to do what you say no matter what.

A big part of positive discipline is making children aware of how their actions have an effect on other people's feelings and emotions. So you basically want to develop their emotional intelligencer as this will in turn help develop their moral compass. This means that they will make better decisions about their behavior all by themselves.

So all of this is probably sounding pretty good right now isn't it? All of these benefits with no yelling? Well I'm not going to lie, it's not easy to achieve, but it's definitely worth it.

Implementing Positive Discipline

In order to start implementing positive discipline into your child's life, you need to start by implementing it into yours. It's more about working on yourself than working on your child. You have to change the way you react and the way you use and view discipline. Then your child will learn as a result of these changes that you will be making to yourself. You have to lead by example.

Understanding

It's important that you do your best to understand the mentality behind the behavior that your children are displaying. Trying to gain a deeper understanding of their behavior will also lead you to not jump to immediate conclusions and get angry so quickly.

It's our job as parents do work out why our children are doing what they are doing. If they are acting up, there is going to be a reason behind it, so rather than being angry with them, do your very best to understand what is making them act this way.

Once you have identified why the child is acting this way, you can address the root of the problem directly. By removing this root issue and taking care of it you will not only be stopping the need for the child to misbehave but you will also be strengthening your bond and connection with your child. If you show that you are there to help them and won't just get angry all the time, they will feel much closer to you and they will show you more of that all-important respect.

Giving Attention

Everyone knows that children sometimes misbehave simply to get their parents attention. This means that it's vital to also give attention at the times that children display favorable behavior. Or even better, give them even more attention when they are behaving as you would like and less attention when they aren't.

Most people tend to ignore their children a bit when they are being good whether they admit it or not. If they are behaving, you can get on with other things that need doing so it makes sense that you wouldn't give them as much attention during this time. Just try and make a bit more time to give them attention when they are behaving and keep this in mind.

Also, if your child is playing up by yelling and throwing their toys about for example, you can always try walking away. There will then be no reasons for them to act that way as there is no one watching. Before long they will learn that this disruptive behavior isn't really achieving anything.

Don't Bribe

There's nothing wrong with treating your child to something nice every now and again. But don't use anything to bribe them into behaving. Doing this will give off the impression that you know they want to misbehave, and that's fine as long as they don't act upon it. You want them to not want to misbehave for the right reasons, not because they are being rewarded not to.

FINAL THOUGHTS

Well I think that about covers it! So now you should have a pretty good idea of why stopping yelling is so important and how to actually stop. If you follow the guide, this is something that is very achievable, especially when combined with the extra tips and tricks that I have provided.

Also the information on positive discipline should also provide some new ideas on how to react to issues rather than simply yelling at your kids in future.

Thank you so much for reading this book, I really appreciate it. If you would also consider taking the time to leave me an honest review on this book on Amazon I would be extremely appreciative of your feedback.

You can find links to all of my previous books full of great advice for women by simply searching for "Amelia Farris" on Amazon. Thanks again for reading and I hopefully speak to you all in the next book!

Made in the USA
Coppell, TX
14 March 2020